POEMS … S

r

SPRING

by

Mary Fleeson

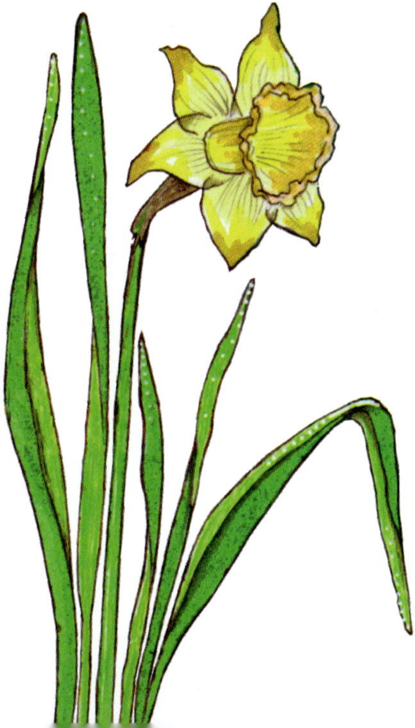

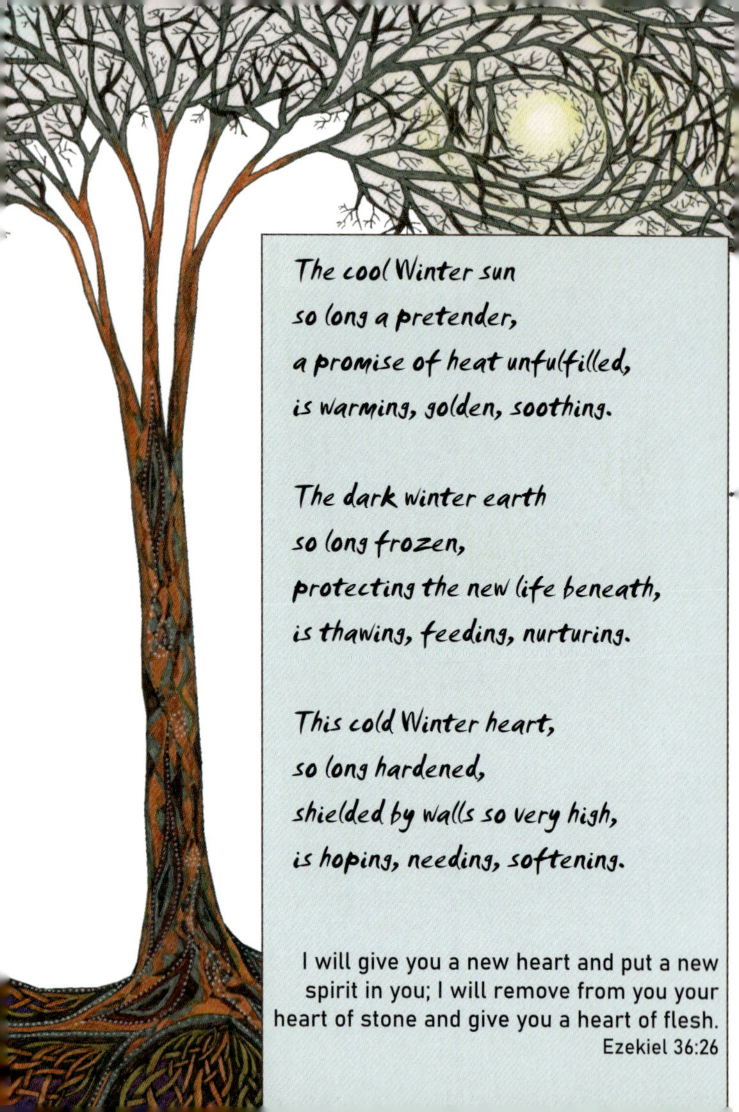

The cool Winter sun
so long a pretender,
a promise of heat unfulfilled,
is warming, golden, soothing.

The dark winter earth
so long frozen,
protecting the new life beneath,
is thawing, feeding, nurturing.

This cold Winter heart,
so long hardened,
shielded by walls so very high,
is hoping, needing, softening.

I will give you a new heart and put a new spirit in you; I will remove from you your heart of stone and give you a heart of flesh.
Ezekiel 36:26

Distant fields,
throwing off the shroud of chilly mist at last!
As the plants grow may my faith grow,
May I trust You more.

Dormant branches,
stretch out new shoots towards the sun.
As the leaves grow may my love grow,
May I love You more.

Longer days,
the darkness of night retreats defeated.
As the light shines on Your creation,
May I reflect Your light.

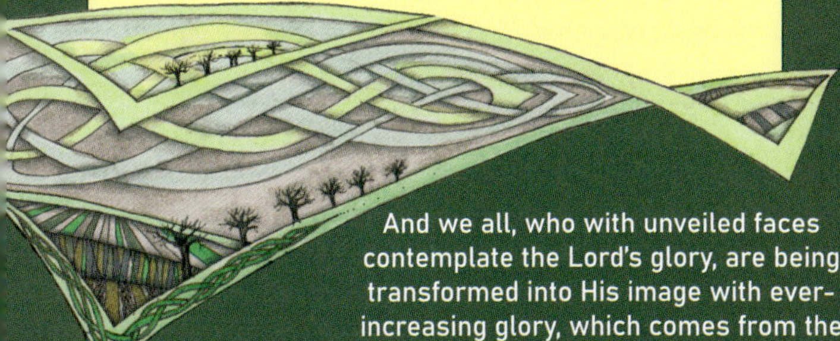

And we all, who with unveiled faces contemplate the Lord's glory, are being transformed into His image with ever-increasing glory, which comes from the Lord, who is the Spirit. 2 Corinthians 3:18

Distant horizon
telescope magnified
examine in sharp detail
precocious shoots of green
hopeful symbols of life abundant...

This small life
wonderfully made
nurture with unlimited love
protect this precious spirit of mine
bless and keep its fragile temple home.

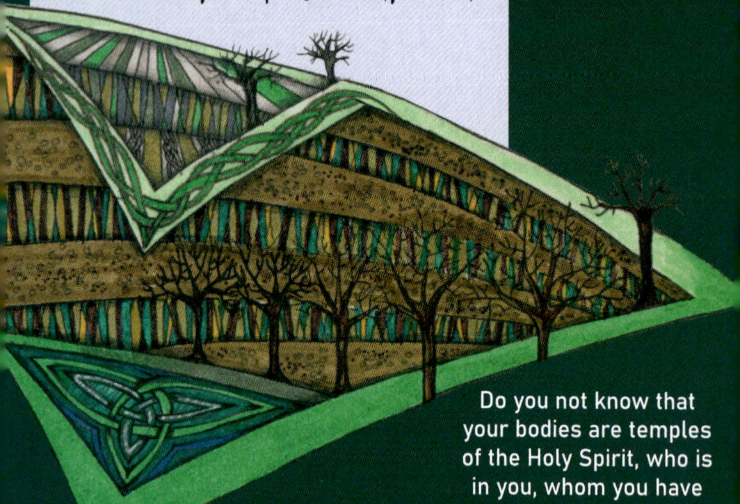

Do you not know that
your bodies are temples
of the Holy Spirit, who is
in you, whom you have
received from God?
1 Corinthians 6:19

To My Many Demands,

I am addressing you today to say, enough!
Enough jostling and pushing,
shouting and rushing.
I've had enough!
My mind, my body and my spirit
belong to my Creator God.
Don't push God around.

Each commitment, plan and chore,
take a ticket and wait in line,
you'll be sorted, you'll be fine.
Just going to take my time!
My mind, my body and my spirit
belong to my Creator God.
And God comes first.

Remain in Me, as I also remain in you. No branch can bear fruit by itself; it must remain in the vine. Neither can you bear fruit unless you remain in me. John 15:4

Sparrow, sparrow,
Hopping near my toes,
Chattering as he goes.

Sparrow, sparrow,
Sitting on the fence,
A pair for one pence*.

Sparrow, sparrow,
Bathing in the sunlight,
Precious in God's sight.

Sparrow, sparrow,
Sing a song for me,
High up in the tree.

Loving God,
hear my chattering prayer,
help me to listen in return.

Loving God,
help me to make good choices,
and believe I am valued.

Loving God,
let me rest in Your light,
Keep the darkness away.

Loving God,
I want to praise You,
And lift my voice to You.

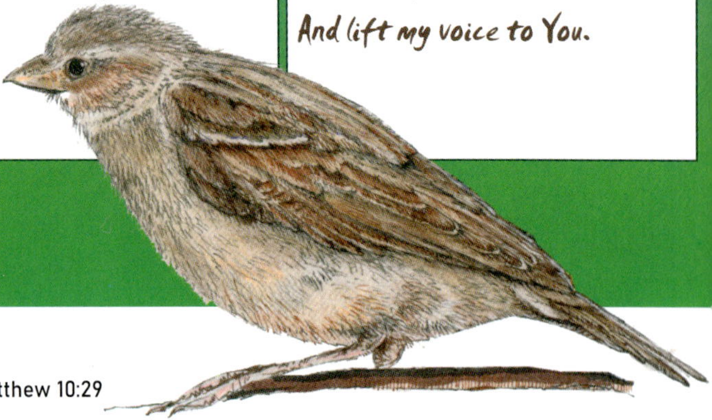

*Matthew 10:29

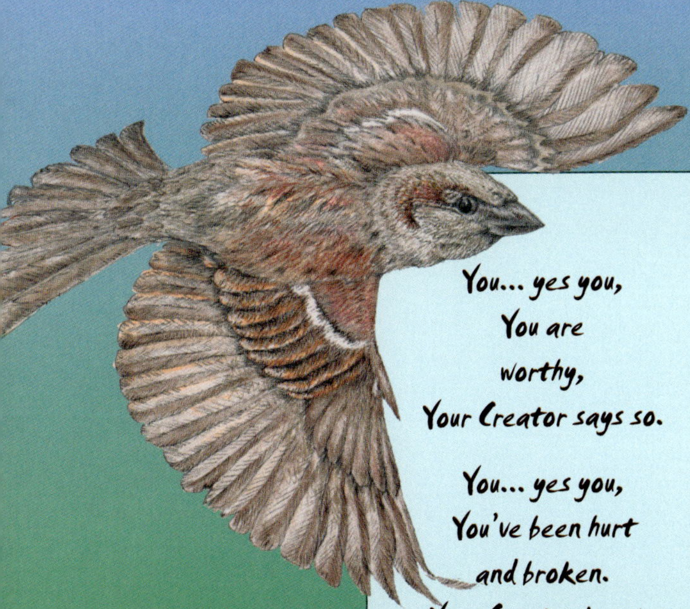

You... yes you,
You are
worthy,
Your Creator says so.

You... yes you,
You've been hurt
and broken.
Your Creator knows.

You... yes, you,
You are
loved...
Your Creator proved it.

You... yes you,
Hold on to the
strong hand...
Your Creator is beside you.

So don't be afraid; you are worth more than many sparrows.
Matthew 10:31

Late Spring, almost Summer
and the shop door is open wide,
the sun warms the wooden floor
and a warm welcome waits inside.

A newly flying, curious sparrow
hops up the step and takes a look.
Where is the sky, the grass and bush?
He flies then settles on a book.

I, the sparrow-whisperer,
Return him to the trees,
Release him from my gentle hands,
To the sea-scented breeze.

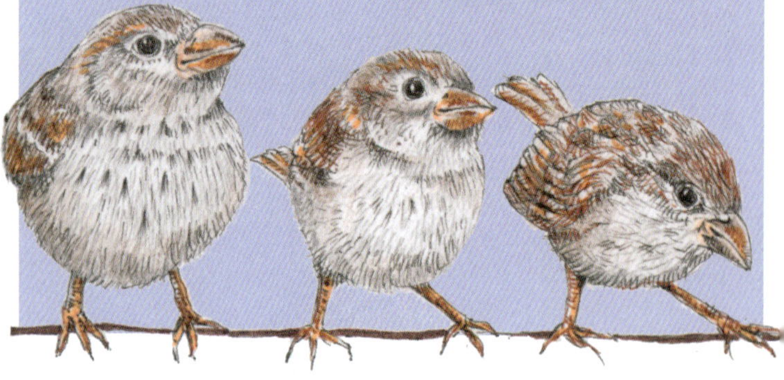

Late Spring, almost Summer
and my life is open wide,
the Son warms my hardened heart,
My prayers invite His Spirit inside.

A newly flying, curious me
wants all the answers in one look.
Where is the hope, the truth and love?
I flutter and settle on The Book.

God, the human-saviour,
Let me understand this life, please,
Hold me in Your gentle hands, refresh me
More than this gentle breeze.

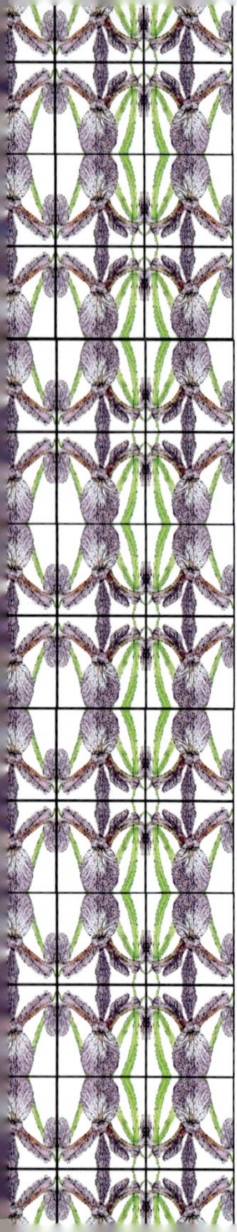

O God, that I may stop and see a flower
and consider Your provision for my life,
Instead of 'will it make me sneeze?'

O God, that I may stop and see a bird
and consider Your attention to detail,
Instead of 'I don't matter.'

O God, that I may stop and see You in all
and consider Your presence around me,
Instead of 'I'm too busy to stop!'

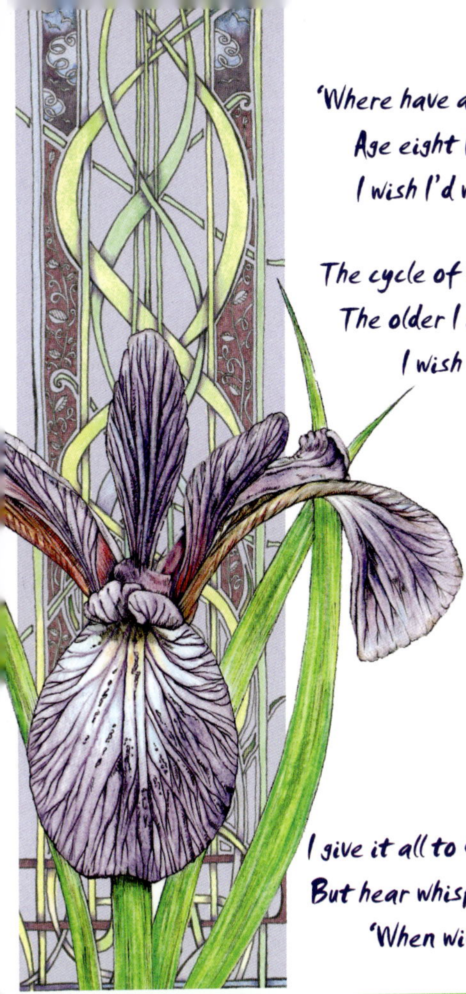

'Where have all the flowers gone?'
Age eight I learnt the song,
I wish I'd written the lines.

The cycle of life turns and turns,
The older I get the less I know
I wish I understood.

I give it all to God in faith and hope
But hear whispered the wry refrain
'When will we ever learn?'

Whatever is has already been before; and God will call the past to account. Ecclesiastes 3:15

Spring wouldn't be Spring,
in this part of the world,
without Easter.
The wondrous, pain-filled sacrifice,
the penultimate chapter
of an extraordinary life,
the celebration and mourning
of God become man.

Easter wouldn't be Easter
anywhere,
without Love.
The love that held Jesus to a cross,
the sacrificial love
of an extraordinary man.
The love of the Creator-Father
who made this world.

Circle us Creator God with the
hope of Spring,
may the presence of Your Spirit grow
in the field of our awareness like the
seeds sprouting from the earth.
Circle us Creator God
with the hope of Spring,
may we grow in faith,
may we grow in love,
may we grow in Your presence.

I remember the smells and sounds of Springs gone by,
Damp turned earth and excited birdsong,
Chilly mornings gently warming,
Sudden showers of icy rain...

I remember the sights and feel of Springs gone by,
Banks of daffodils and soft chicks,
Afternoon walks by the shore,
Windows open wide...

Moments that seem so ordinary
May define a whole time of life.
Memories are precious,
And yet even these may fade.

Our Spring of today,
Newly growing, freshly begun,
Is where we are called to live.
In the here and now.

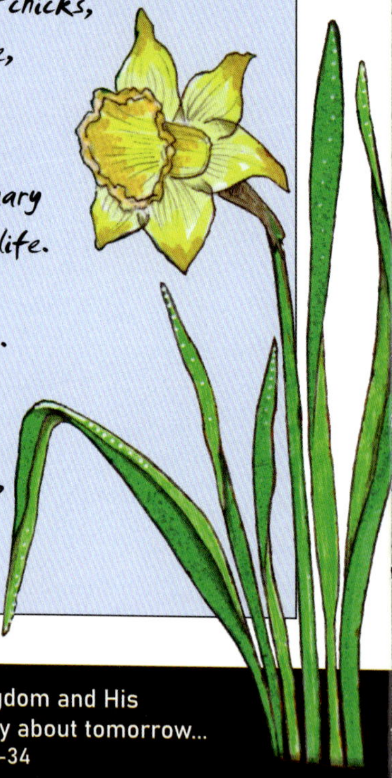

But seek first His kingdom and His righteousness... do not worry about tomorrow...
Matthew 6:33–34

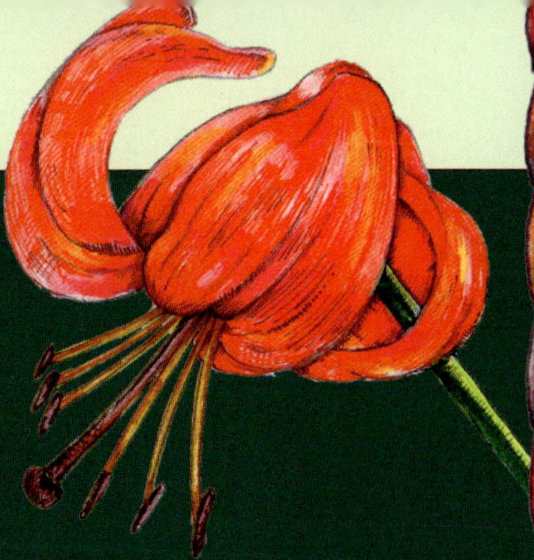

The season turns,
blooms mature,
colours deepen,
blossom falls,
fruits ripen.

Where once we could excuse ourselves,
plead ignorance or youth,
now our hearts and minds
cannot unsee, cannot unhear,
the cries from the world.

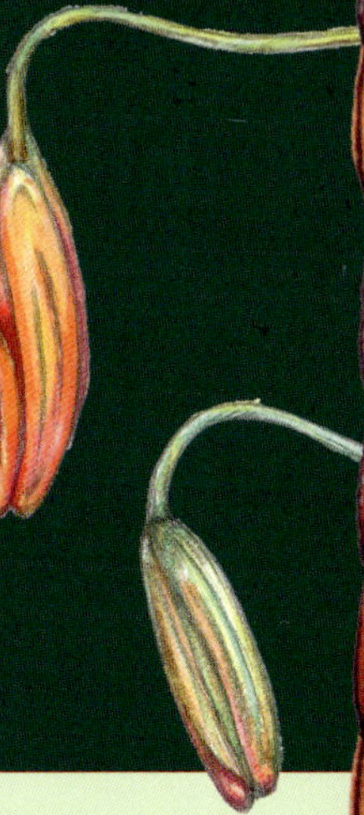

Let our faith be real,
Let our hearts be open,
Let our hands be willing to do Your will.

When I was a child, I used to speak like a child,
think like a child, reason like a child; when I became a man,
I did away with childish things.
1 Corinthians 13:11

The Spring sun through the window pane warms my Winter-dried hand as I draw a curving line upon the unblemished virgin page.

From the snow-white sheet knotted ribbon emerges like swirling eddies of sea-water around the posts of the old pier.

Under and over repeated again and again then colours picked and placed with care with words that speak of God and love.

I stretch my fingers and back and toes and I know I've sat too long hardly breathing and praying silently for you.